ANCIENT CHINA

by Robert Nicholson and Claire Watts

Editorial Consultant: Dr Anne Farrer,
Department of Oriental Antiquities, British Museum

TWO-CAN

First published in Great Britain in 1991 by
Two-Can Publishing Ltd
346 Old Street
London EC1V 9NQ

Printed in Hong Kong

4 6 8 10 9 7 5 3

British Library Cataloguing in Publication Data
Nicholson, Roberts
    Ancient China
    1. China, ancient period
    I. Title II. Watts, Claire III. Series
    931

ISBN: 1-85434-014-X

Photographic credits:
Werner Forman: p.1, p.8, p.9, p.11, p.20, p.24, p.30(c); Sonia Halliday: p.5, p.13; Toby
Maudsley: p.17, p.23; Ronald Sheridan: p.11, p.12, p.15, p.18, p.19(l), p.21; John Stevens:
p.30(t), p.30(b); E T Archive: p.19; Zefa: p.6, p.7

Illustration credits:
Jon Davis/Linden Artists: p.4; Malcolm Stokes/Linden Artists: p.6, p.8, p.9, p.10, p.12, p.14,
p.15, p.16, p.17, p.18, p.20, p.21, p.22, p.24; Maxine Hamil: Cover, pp 25-29

Contents

All words in **bold** can be found in the glossary

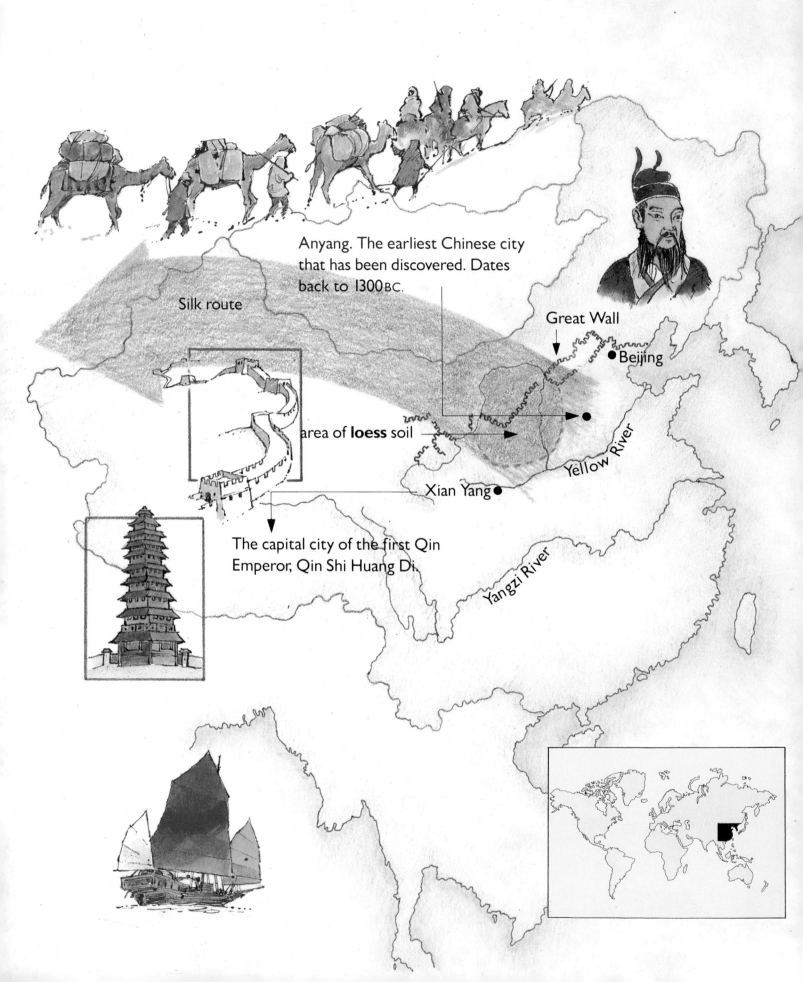

Anyang. The earliest Chinese city that has been discovered. Dates back to 1300 BC.

Silk route

Great Wall

Beijing

area of **loess** soil

Yellow River

Xian Yang

The capital city of the first Qin Emperor, Qin Shi Huang Di.

Yangzi River

The Ancient Chinese World

China was a united country with big cities and a system of government, before the great European **civilisations**, the Greeks and the Romans, had even begun to spread across Europe. One family grew so powerful that it managed to take over the lands of local lords by about 1766BC and continued to rule for 700 years. Other families have ruled China throughout its history. The period of time when one family ruled is known as a **dynasty**. One of the most famous is the Qin dynasty, which China is named after.

Chinese Lands

China is a huge country, stretching over 3,000 km from the mountains and ice of Tibet in the west through forests and deserts to the tropical coastline of the east.

Chinese civilisation first began around the Yellow River in the centre of the country, where the soil is a rich yellow earth called loess. This fertile earth has been blown on to the land by the wind over thousands of years.

The ancient Chinese discovered that they could grow good crops on this loess only if it was kept well watered. They developed a system of **terraces** cut into the hillsides to make the most of the land. In the north, wheat was the main crop, and in the south, where there was more water, rice was grown in flooded paddy-fields.

Peasant farmers provided food for the whole of the huge Chinese empire but often they had scarcely enough to eat themselves. Crops often failed causing periods of great famine. The starving peasants sometimes rebelled against the rich landlords.

▲ Complex irrigation systems were set up to water the fields.

▶ Terraces were cut into the hillsides to make the most of every bit of land.

The Great Wall

The Great Wall of China was built to protect China's northern border from invading tribes. In 221 BC the new emperor Qin Shi Huang Di sent 30,000 men to start building the wall. From then on emperor after emperor extended and rebuilt it right up to this century. The wall was made of pounded earth covered with stones. It was wide at the bottom and narrowed at the top, where there was a walkway for guards. The length of the wall was broken at intervals by watchtowers.

▲ Traders used to travel along China's northern border, taking their **silk** to India, the Middle East and Europe.

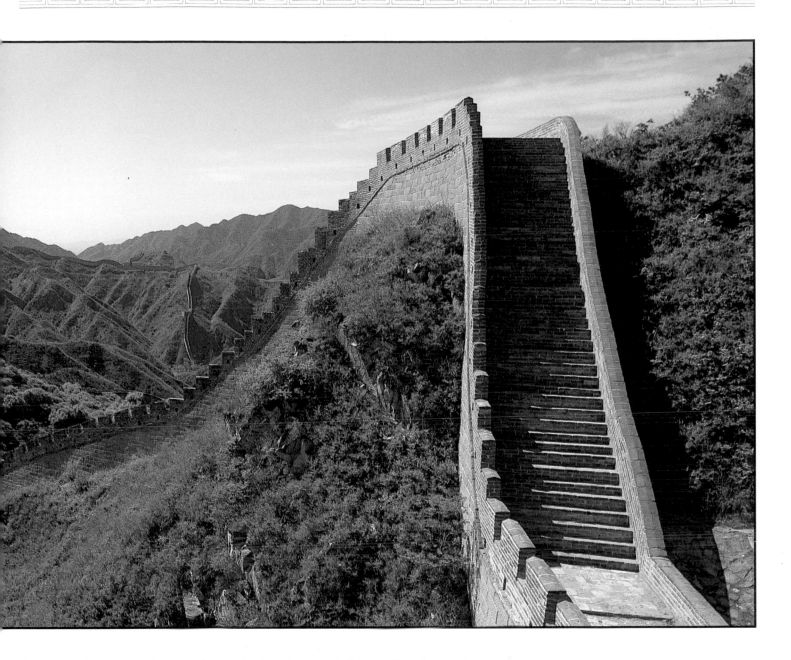

▲ According to a Chinese legend, the Great Wall is really a huge dragon turned to stone.

Great Wall Facts

● The wall is between 5m and 10m high.
● The walkway along the top is 5m wide.
● Watch-towers are located every 90m to 180m along the wall.
● The wall originally stretched for 6,000km along China's border.

▶ Cross-section of the Great Wall.

The Forbidden City

China was one of the first countries in the world to have large numbers of people living close to one another in cities. Chinese cities were built with walls all around them to protect them from enemies. Inside the most important city of China the emperor had a palace which also had high walls, like a city within a city.

In the Ming dynasty, the emperor Yongle rebuilt China's main city, Beijing. By this time

Beijing had a million inhabitants. Inside the city walls was a walled imperial city where the important government officials lived and worked. Inside this area was a palace known as the Forbidden City where the emperor lived. The Forbidden City was surrounded by a 12m wide moat, and walls 12m high and 12m thick. At night no man other than the Emperor was allowed inside.

▼ In the Qin dynasty, coins were introduced. The coins were round with holes in the middle.

Government

The first Chinese emperors gave huge estates to their friends and relatives all over China in the hope that this would help them govern the country effectively. However, these lords often became too strong for the Emperor to control, and civil war followed. In the Qin dynasty, the emperors began to set up a form of **civil service** to govern the country instead. People who wanted to join the civil service had to take very difficult exams to prove that they could do the job.

▼ People walking along the long, straight road to the Forbidden City could be seen long before they arrived at the gates.

City Life

The Chinese believed that the world was square, so they built their cities to reflect this, laid out in regular patterns, with straight streets crossing each other at right angles. This divided the town into squares, known as *wards*. Usually the houses of the rich would be found at one end, near the palace, and those of the poor at the other end.

The poor people had houses built from mud and thatch. To keep out draughts in winter, the houses were built with floors below ground level, and blankets were hung over the windows and doors. In the centre of the house was a sunken pit containing the fire, but there was no chimney to let out the smoke.

Rich people's houses were built around huge courtyards. They were made of painted wood, roofed with pottery tiles. They contained little furniture – straw mattresses which were rolled up during the day, cushions rather than chairs, and big chests and cupboards.

▼ Chinese houses had curved roofs designed to keep away evil spirits. Spirits were believed to travel in straight lines and it was thought that the curved roofs would confuse them!

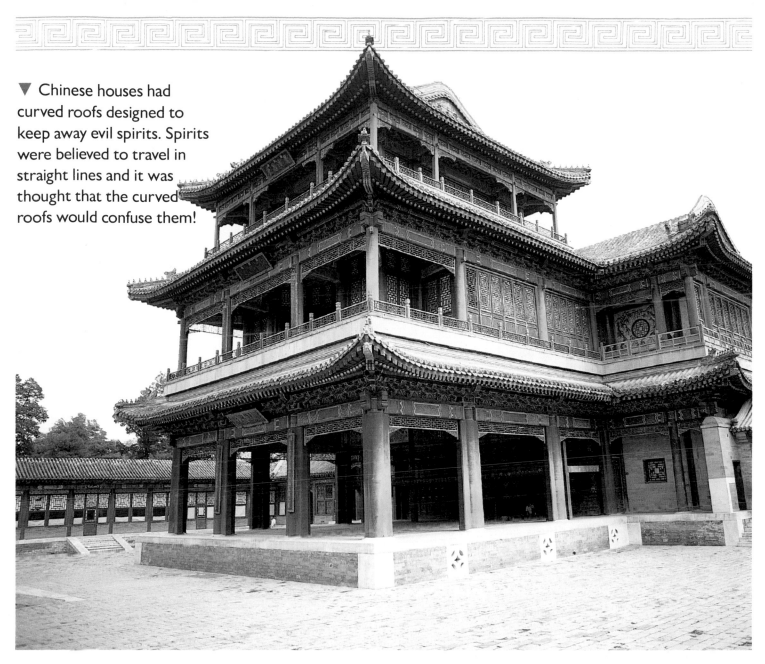

Festivals

Most Chinese people worked very hard and had no regular days off or weekends. Instead there were festivals throughout the year, which were celebrated with processions and dancing in the street. Fireworks would be let off, kites flown, and people would dress up in dragon costumes, as dragons were supposed to represent fun and excitement.

▶ Dragons and other grotesque creatures were supposed to protect the house and bring good luck.

13

Inventions

Chinese scientists discovered many things that have made great changes to civilisation throughout the world. They were interested in medicine, navigation, chemistry, and, of course, they were always trying to improve agriculture to feed the enormous population.

Fireworks and Rockets

Chinese inventors discovered the correct formula to make **gunpowder**. This was first used to make fire bombs. It is likely that they also made the earliest cannons.

The Wheelbarrow

The Chinese invented all sorts of lifting apparatus, including the wheelbarrow, which they called a wooden ox.

Compass

The Chinese discovered magnetism and made **compasses** by floating magnets in bowls of water. These were used for navigation, and to check that a new building faced in a direction which would bring good fortune.

Medicine

Chinese doctors were very good at treating various illnesses. They invented some cures which are still used today, like *kaolin*, made from powdered clay, for an upset stomach. They often treated illness with **acupuncture**. Needles were stuck into the skin in particular places on the body to cure problems in other parts of the body. Many people still use acupuncture today to help with certain illnesses.

▼ Doctors had to know exactly where in the body to place one of these needles to help their patients.

▲ This huge water wheel would power the giant water clock.

Clockwork

Clockwork was another Chinese invention. Giant water clocks were invented which rang every 15 minutes to record the passing of the day for the royal officials. The records of this invention were kept so carefully that modern clock-makers have been able to use them to reconstruct the clocks.

Paper

Perhaps the greatest Chinese invention of all was paper and with it, printing.

The earliest Chinese writing has been found carved on animal bones. After this, the Chinese began to paint on bamboo strips and silk. In about 100AD paper was invented. Wood pulp, hemp and other waste material were mashed up, mixed with water, rolled, stretched and dried in the sun to form paper. Paper was the cheapest writing material, and it was much quicker and easier to write on than anything people had used before.

Within a few hundred years the Chinese had developed a form of printing. Wooden blocks carved with lines of text were rubbed over with ink and then paper was smoothed on to them. This was very much quicker than writing books by hand and copies could be made very easily.

Chinese Writing

Chinese letters are different from ours. Each of our letters represents a sound, and for them to mean anything we have to combine them to make up a word. Chinese letters are called *characters*. They do not represent sounds but meanings. At first some characters were pictures which could very easily be understood, but gradually the signs became simpler, to make them quicker and easier to write.

EARLY CHARACTERS	MODERN	ENGLISH
𖤥	山	mountain
⊖	日	sun
⊃	月	moon
𥝱	馬	horse

Cutting reeds and soaking them.

Mashing the pulp.

Make Your Own Printing Block

The ancient Chinese carved their printing blocks out of wood, but here's an easier way of doing it! Draw a design and trace it. Cut several copies of the design out of card and glue them, one on top of another on to a piece of stiff card, so that the design is raised above the surface. Cover your printing block with ink or paint and press onto a sheet of paper.

Always ask a grown-up to help you when you use sharp scissors.

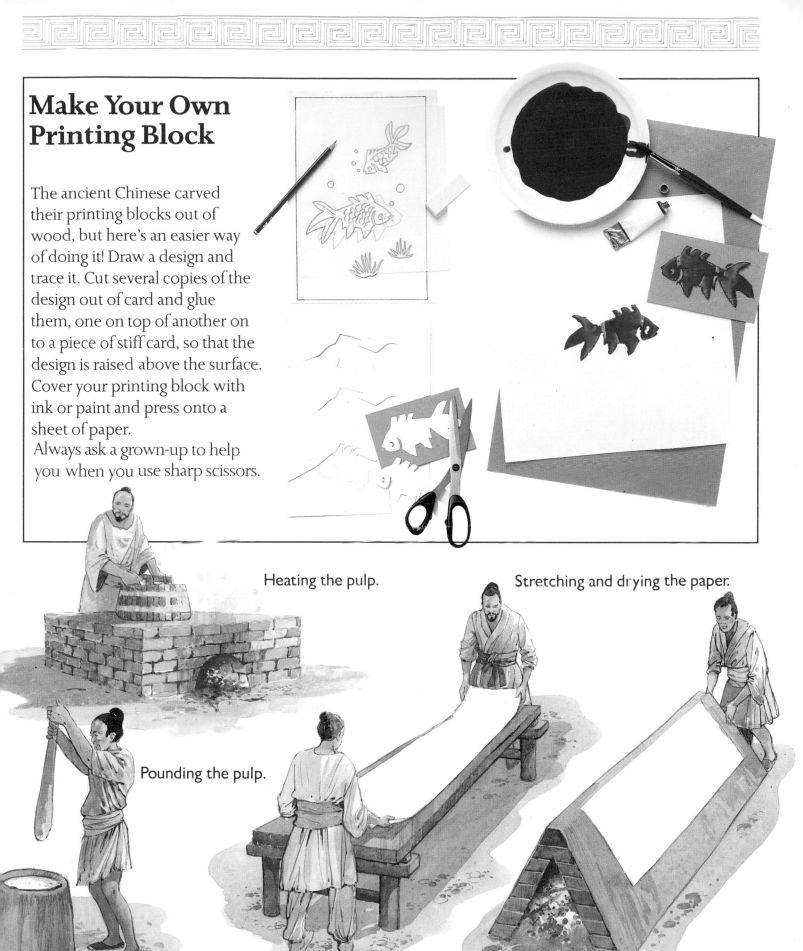

Heating the pulp.

Stretching and drying the paper.

Pounding the pulp.

Great Thinkers

The Chinese have never believed in a single all-powerful god, and the government never tried to force the people to believe in one religion. People believed that different religious beliefs would all fit together quite well. Most Chinese people believed that the balance of nature was delicate and that everything had an opposite side which was very important. They called the two opposite forces which governed everything **yin and yang**. A balance of these was thought to bring peace, joy and order.

Buddhism

Buddha taught people that they should free themselves of all worldly desires in order to gain perfect happiness or *nirvana*. **Buddhism,** which originally came from India, became China's most popular religion.

Daoism

Confucius thought that people were the most important element in the world, but another great thinker, **Lao Zi,** developed **Daoism.** This taught that people were only one element among thousands which make up the world and that they should try to fit in with the ways of the universe rather than change it.

Kong Zi

The most famous Chinese **philosopher, Kong Zi** (often known as Confucius), lived in the Zhou dynasty. He taught that people could only live together happily and peacefully if they followed the rules which he set down in a book called the **Analects**. He believed that it was very important to respect other people, and one of his teachings was *do to other people as you would like them to do to you*. The teachings of Confucius developed into the empire's main religion.

Craft

The Chinese were experts in many crafts. They produced beautiful objects in metal, stone and pottery.

Jade

Jade is a hard green stone which was considered very valuable by the Chinese. They believed it represented five essential virtues: charity, trustworthiness, courage, wisdom and fairness. This funeral suit is made from 2,000 pieces of jade threaded together with gold-covered wire.

China

The Chinese invented a form of light pottery or **porcelain** which we still call *china*. They decorated it with delicate patterns and colours.

20

Gardens

Gardening was regarded as a great art. Chinese cities were designed to include peaceful gardens and parks. Each item in the garden was thought to have a different meaning: water-lilies represented truth, chrysanthemums, culture, and bamboo, strength.

Silk

The Chinese kept the secret of silk-making to themselves for many years. Silk thread comes from the cocoon of a type of caterpillar, which has to be carefully cared for and fed on mulberry leaves. The cloth made from this thread was the source of China's trade with other countries.

Lacquer

Lacquer is made from the sap of a special type of oak tree. When heated, the sap becomes hard and shiny like glass. It was used with dyes to decorate houses and furniture.

Food

Rich Chinese people ate exciting and varied food, much like the Chinese food we know today. They ate a wide variety of meat, like ox, mutton, deer, pig and even dog. The most common dish was a rich stew called *geng*. Meals contained lots of small courses and sometimes a big feast would go on for half a day. There might be 300 different dishes to choose from at a feast including delicacies like bears' paws, baked owl and birds' nest soup.

Poor people often struggled to eat enough to stay alive. Their geng usually contained only vegetables. People in the north ate a lot of a cereal called millet, and in the south they ate rice. They also ate beancurd, noodles and bread.

Food was eaten out of small bowls using chopsticks and weak green tea was drunk with it. The rich drank wine made from rice.

Cooking

Most Chinese food is cooked very quickly to preserve the different flavours and textures of all the different meats and finely chopped vegetables. Lots of separate dishes are served at once.

Root ginger

Noodles

Chinese leaves

Bean curd

Rice

▲ Although poor Chinese people ate mostly bland rice and beancurd they added strong flavoured spices and ginger to them to make them taste better.

23

Clothes

Rich and poor people in China wore very different clothes. Poor men would wear baggy hemp trousers, with a loose shirt over the top and a fur-lined coat in winter. The women wore simple dresses made from wool in winter and cotton in summer. Their shoes were made from woven straw.

Rich men and women wore robes of silk tied at the waist with a large sash. The front of a woman's robe was opened a little to reveal an undershirt of different coloured silk. They wore silk slippers with wooden soles on their feet.

▼ This embroidered badge would have been worn by an official to show his rank.

▲ Silk clothes were often beautifully embroidered with scenes from stories or lucky symbols.

Small babies were carried on their mother's back in a fold of her dress until they were old enough to walk. From then on they wore miniature versions of adult clothes.

Both men and women had long hair. Most people wore this in a topknot, but rich women had their hair dressed in elaborate shapes and decorated with jewelled combs. People only cut their hair when a close family member had died.

The Dragon King's Key

The ancient Chinese told many stories about the world around them. Although these stories are not true we can find out about life in ancient China from them. The Dragon King's Key is a tale about a drought.

The rains around Horse Ear Mountain were very poor one year. The land was so dry that the crops would not grow and the people who lived at the foot of the mountain had nothing to eat. The river dried up and people began to think that they would have to leave their homes or die.

One day, when she was walking on the mountain, a farmer's daughter called Sea Girl came upon a secret lake. She could see the lake shining between the mountain peaks, and smell the cool breeze that rippled its surface, but she could not reach the water.

As she stared longingly at the lake, a wild goose flew down beside her.

"I am the Guardian of the Lake," said the wild goose. "It is impossible to reach the shining waters. They are locked in with a golden key which is hidden in a fortress far away."

"Where can I find the golden key?" Sea Girl cried, but the wild goose flew off without answering. Sea Girl stamped her foot impatiently. "What am I to do?"

Three parrots sitting in a nearby tree heard her cries. They put their heads on one side and stared at her with beady eyes.

"If you want the key…" said one in a rather bored voice.

"…you must search for…" the second continued, yawning.

"…the Third Daughter…" The last parrot spoke so slowly that Sea Girl thought he would fall asleep before he finished.

"…of the …Dragon King." Then the three parrots tucked their heads under their wings and fell asleep before Sea Girl had a chance to ask them any more.

"But who is the Dragon King, and where should I look for his daughter?" she wailed.

Sea Girl looked around but no other bird or creature came to help her.

"I shall just have to find the Third Daughter of the Dragon King by myself."

So Sea Girl set off, singing a song about her quest. Many people stopped her along the way to ask about her song, but none could tell her of the Third Daughter of the Dragon King.

After many long and tiring days of walking, Sea Girl met a peacock.

"I have heard your song, Sea Girl," said the peacock. "I know the fortress far away in the Southern Mountains where the Dragon King lives. I will take you there."

Sea Girl thanked the peacock and set off after him, singing her song as she went. She followed him to the crags of the Southern Mountains. There she saw a huge fortress guarded by a fierce and monstrous eagle with huge talons and a pointed beak.

"Here I must leave you," said the peacock. "This is where the Dragon King lives with his daughters. I cannot tell you how to get into the fortress, but I do know that the Third Daughter of the Dragon King loves music. Perhaps if you sing, something will happen."

Sea Girl sat outside the fortress and began to sing. On the first day, she sang all the songs she knew, but the Third Daughter of the Dragon King did not appear. On the second day, she sang all the songs she knew again. Staring up at the fortress, she thought she glimpsed a girl's face at one of the windows. On the third day, Sea Girl started to make up new songs. She sang all day and at last, as the Sun began to set, the Third Daughter of the Dragon King appeared beside her. Sea Girl carried on with her songs. Shyly the other girl joined in, and soon the mountain was filled with the sound of the two friends' voices.

Sea Girl explained her quest to Third Daughter, and Third Daughter agreed to help.

She told Sea Girl that the golden key to the secret lake was kept in the left hand dungeon of the fortress. To reach the dungeon Sea Girl would have to pass the monstrous eagle.

"But how am I to get past him?" said Sea Girl.

"I have an idea..." Third Daughter replied, and began to explain her plan.

Sea Girl and Third Daughter sang very loudly until the monstrous eagle who guarded the fortress flew over to see what was happening. Third Daughter kept singing, lulling the eagle with her sweet voice, while Sea Girl stole away and crept into the fortress.

The left hand dungeon was filled with piles of treasure. But Sea Girl turned her back on the gold, jade and jewels and began to look for the key. She spotted it glinting in a dark corner. Clutching the key, she ran from the fortress and made her way back to Third Daughter.

When Sea Girl was safely clear of the fortress Third Daughter stopped singing. The monstrous eagle flew back to the fortress. He did not realise that the golden key was missing because the heaps of gold, jade and jewels that he guarded had not been disturbed.

Sea Girl returned to Horse Ear Mountain with the key. She went to the shining lake and opened it with the golden key. Immediately the water began to flow down from the lake into the river that ran through the village.

From his fortress in the Southern Mountains the Dragon King saw what had happened. He was furious. When he found out how Third Daughter had helped Sea Girl, he banished her from his kingdom forever.

Third Daughter was not very upset by this. Life had been very dull in the Dragon King's fortress, and she had been forbidden to sing. So she went

to Horse Ear Mountain to live with Sea Girl and the two girls spent their days singing together.

As for the villagers, when they saw the water flowing into their river, they rushed out of their houses, laughing and crying. They were very grateful to the two girls. One day in every year the ladies of Horse Ear Mountain still sing together by the river to thank Sea Girl and Third Daughter.

29

How We Know

Have you ever wondered how we know so much about the lives of the ancient Chinese, although they lived thousands of years ago?

Evidence from the Ground

Chinese emperors and important officials were often buried in elaborate tombs which contained many everyday objects. Archaeologists can find out a lot about the way these people lived by studying these objects. One tomb contained a life-size army – 6,000 pottery soldiers and horses, each one with a different face.

Evidence from Books

The Chinese emperors developed a huge administrative system to run their country, and detailed records were made of everything that went on. Many of these records still exist.

▲ The pottery army was an extremely useful find for archaeologists.

◀ Records come in all shapes and sizes. This writing is on wood.

▼ An emperor was still living in the Forbidden City up until 1911, so most of it is beautifully preserved.

Evidence around Us

Many of the things created by the ancient Chinese survive. The country is still divided into the 18 provinces. The Forbidden City and other palaces still stand to tell us much about Chinese architecture. Acupuncture and other forms of medicine invented by the ancient Chinese are still used today.

Glossary

acupuncture
the treatment of illness by sticking small needles into specific places on a person's body.

Analects
the collection of Kong Zi's philosophical writings.

Buddhism
the teachings of the Indian prophet Buddha, who died in 483 BC.

civil service
the government departments, such as the treasury, which administrate the country.

civilisation
an organised society which has developed social customs, government, technology and the arts.

compass
an instrument for showing direction, which works by means of magnetism.

Daoism
the belief that life should be lived in harmony with nature.

dynasty
a series of rulers all belonging to the same family. The dynasties mentioned in this book are:

Zhou	1027–256 BC
Qin	221–206 BC
Ming	1368–1644 BC

gunpowder
a powder which explodes when lit.

hemp
a plant producing a coarse thread, often used to make rope and sacking.

jade
a hard green stone used for making jewellery and ornaments.

Kong Zi
China's most famous philosopher, who lived in the Zhou dynasty. Often known as Confucius in western countries.

lacquer
a shiny coating used to decorate wood.

Lao Zi
Chinese philosopher who lived in the Zhou dynasty.

loess
a fertile yellow topsoil.

philosopher
a learned person who thinks up new ways to look at the world. Philosophers are particularly concerned with religious beliefs and society.

porcelain
a fine china used to make crockery and ornaments.

silk
a fine, soft cloth made from a thread produced by silkworms.

terraces
flat fields built like steps into the side of a hill to stop the soil from sliding away.

yin and yang
Chinese symbols which suggest the opposite sides of nature and together mean balance.

Index